To my husband,
Quinn, for filling me with laughter and encouraging me to finish this book. You are the true yogi of the family.

And to the children reading,
remember to find joy and magic from everyone and everything around you.

The light in me sees the light in you.

Note to the parents and readers of this book:

The poses in this book are all based
on traditional yoga poses, with some
names simplified for children.
While reading this book,
try practicing the poses with Lily
as she meets different friends in nature.
Lily's adventure is not only a great story,
but an introduction to yoga you can try
at home while you read again and again!

The word "Om" is a spiritual sound and
symbol highly associated with yoga.
You often chant this mantra at the
beginning or end of a yoga class to
help calm the nervous system and
synchronize breath with those around you.
The word Om represents universal oneness
and pure consciousness.

Try saying Om out loud with your child!

Lily Finds Her Om way

A Child's Introduction to Yoga

As they walked, Lily and her grandma walked further and further away from the BUSES, the TAXIS, the BUILDINGS.

The noises began to fade and
Lily and her grandma could hear new sounds—
BIRDS, CRICKETS, WATER.
They came across a pond.

Lily tried it. She plopped down with her legs bent out.

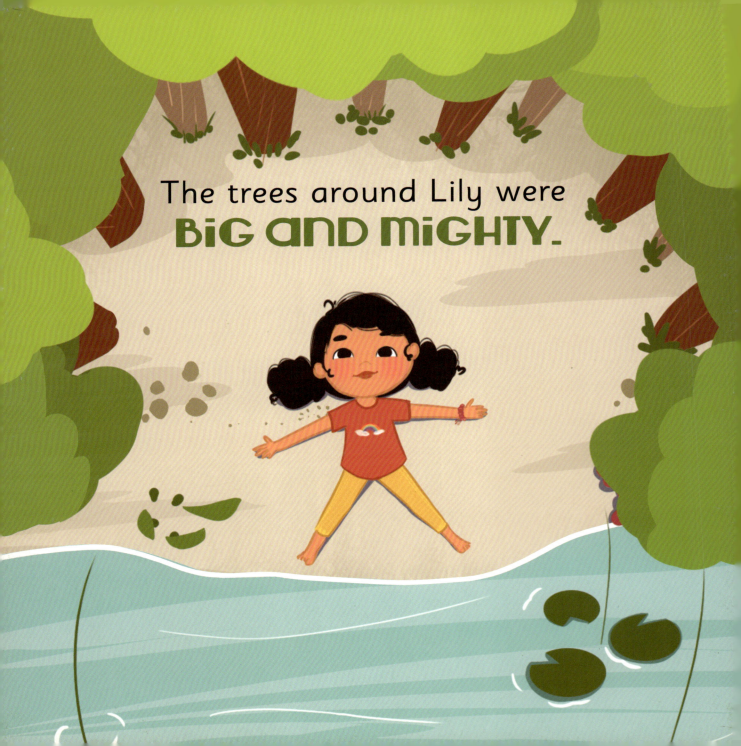

"Tree, what gives you your strength?" she asked.

"My roots grow deep into the ground and they help me stand tall," replied the tree.

Lily stood next to the tree with one foot touching her calf.
She felt like she had grown ten inches taller!

A beautiful butterfly flew around her face.
Lily was getting dizzy!

"Butterfly, what gives you your grace?" she asked.

"I flap my wings gently with ease," said the butterfly.

Lily brought her feet together to make her own wings. She imagined herself flying over the city. Lily was surprised when she saw a snake but before she could panic, the snake smiled.

"Hello, I'm the Green Garden Snake!"
said the reptile.

"Green Garden Snake,
what gives you your speedy ability?"
she asked.

"I slither quickly with
my body behind me."
replied the snake.

Lily lay on her belly and lifted her head up, she felt her body strong behind her. It started to rain, but Lily did not mind.

The sun soared up, and a sparkling rainbow appeared.

"Rainbow, what gives you your sparkle?" Lily said.

"I accept all of the colors on my rainbow," it said.

Together Lily and Granny put their arms over their heads and sent love to everyone of each
SIZE, SHAPE, AND COLOR.

But suddenly...Lily heard something shaking in the bushes. Right before Lily's eyes was...

a **Lion!** But she wasn't afraid.

"Lion, what gives you your power?" Lily asked.

"I roar loudly for everyone to hear me," the Lion responded.

Lily stuck her tongue out and roared.
She felt powerful and wild!

Lily was ready to head home,
she felt tired...happy.
She sat with Grandma and listened
to the gentle huuush of the grass
and the cheep-cheep of a songbird.
She took three deep breaths.

Lily knew that she could find peace at anytime by simply practicing what her friends had taught her. Today, Lily had found her *om* way.

Lilia Karimi is an adventurer, yoga teacher, and entrepreneur. Lilia has been practicing yoga for ten years and is a proponent of spending more time in nature. She is a Cornell graduate and avid hiker, having summited Mount Rainier and Mount Kilimanjaro. Lilia splits her time between Seattle and New York with her husband. You can find Lilia at www.lifebylilia.com or on Instagram @lifebylilia.

Elif Cansu Özen is a Turkish illustrator who specializes in cartoon and animation. She loves working on projects for kids, which allow her to support and encourage children's imagination. Elif gains her inspiration through traveling, meeting new people, and exploring the magical world around her. You can follow her work on Instagram @elif.cansu.ozen.